How to Build Passive Income : A certain guide/tips in Making Money(Online/physical)

Alfred G. Lipscomb

Table of Contents:

Chapter 1

Getting a skill

Obtaining new Skills Can assist you with proceeding to develop expertly and extend your profession open doors. Contingent upon your inclinations, you can acquire new abilities utilising hands-on preparation, additional schooling and supplemental non-scholarly preparation. It's essential to make and comprehend your objectives both for individual and expert development. In this article, we characterise obtained abilities, investigate their significance and audit 10 stages on the best way to gain new abilities all alone.

What are gained abilities?

Obtained abilities will be capacities you master through training and experience. Frequently, obtained abilities can incorporate both hard and delicate abilities, and these capacities might assist you with working on your presentation at work. Delicate abilities are not effectively quantifiable, yet they normally connect with how you deal with your work and team up and speak with others. Hard abilities frequently show that you have a specific specialised capacity, like programming or dissecting information.

Why are gained abilities significant?

Obtaining new abilities can make you more viable in your job and can exhibit your commitment to progress and headway. As you progress your abilities, you may likewise observe that your abilities are adaptable between ventures. Zeroing in on abilities, for example, PC proficiency, cooperation and correspondence might help you while chasing after other vocational interests

Putting resources into yourself.

Instructions to procure new abilities

1. Pick abilities to master

The expertise you pick relies upon your objectives and interests. On the off chance that you're needing to progress at work, consider asking your supervisor for supplemental preparation ideas they think might be valuable for you to learn. On the off chance that you're hoping to begin another vocation, have a go at taking a gander at work postings to see abilities and their expectation to know where to begin in your abilities preparation.

2. Make time to learn

Put away opportunities consistently to master and practice the new abilities you are acquiring. If you're preparing or taking supplemental courses, consider making a timetable to guarantee you're ready to zero in on the material yet in addition ready to go on with your normal day. It's critical to organise this time with the goal that you don't lose centre around the thing you are attempting to accomplish.

3. Become familiar with the basics

Preceding mastering and rehearsing another ability, understanding its set of experiences and impact is useful. Advance however much you can about its starting points, uses and advantages. For instance, while learning another dialect, some find it supportive to know a few things about the root language that it comes from, as various dialects have various guidelines and elocutions. Gathering this data can likewise assist you with adjusting the ability to your more extensive objectives.

4. Pick the instruments to utilise

In the first place, see what apparatuses are accessible to you, then pick the devices that fit best with your learning style. There might be numerous decisions relying upon the abilities you're keen on securing. A few instruments that might be useful are temporary jobs, books, webcasts, studios, classes or a blend of these choices. Picking the best instruments for your learning style helps keep the substance open and connecting as you seek after your new abilities.

5. Make an educational program

Making an educational plan might assist with smoothing out your way of learning and giving knowledge into the subsequent stages. To construct your educational plan, consider arranging your learning undertakings into consecutive envelopes or steps. If you have any desire to make a difficult or draw an opportunity for growth, take a stab at blending your substance to expand concentration and maintenance, for example, perusing an article and watching a video inside a similar learning period. If you find yourself unfit to dominate a segment, think about checking on prior moves toward reviving your insight.

6. Put forth unambiguous objectives

Putting forth objectives to accomplish abilities is likewise a significant stage in gaining some new useful knowledge. Take a stab at making your objectives quantifiable and feasible to abstain from becoming overpowered during the learning stage. Set however many achievements as you'd like, and consider picking a prize for each significant accomplishment, as these can act as inspirations.

7. Share your objectives

Offering your objectives to another person might assist with making various ways for you to learn. Consider offering your objectives to those you confide in to get legit input and help with exploring your inclinations. It can likewise be useful to impart your objectives to somebody who has proactively procured the abilities you're seeking because they could share significant or essential information that can help you later on.

8. Set cutoff times

Setting cutoff times is an incredible method for rehearsing self-responsibility and making a timetable that works for you. Setting cutoff times can likewise help you focus on and monitor your learning timetable to guarantee you complete your achievements on time. You might find that setting cutoff times assists you with centering and eliminating interruptions.

Assuming you need help with setting and keeping up with cutoff times, consider investigating individuals undertaking the executive's applications for your telephone or internet browser. These frequently permit

you to set due dates for related undertakings and focus on things in light of their significance.
The For sure Publication Group includes a different and skilled group of scholars, specialists and informed authorities furnished with Without a doubt information and experiences to convey valuable tips to assist with directing your professional process.
Gaining new abilities can assist you with proceeding to develop expertly and extend your profession open doors. Contingent upon your inclinations, you can acquire new abilities through hands-on preparing, extra schooling and supplemental non-scholarly preparation. It's critical to make and comprehend your objectives both for individual and expert development. In this article, we characterise gained abilities, investigate their significance and audit 10 stages on the most proficient method to secure new abilities all alone.
Perceive how your compensation looks at

Get customised compensation experiences with the To be sure Compensation Mini-computer

What are procured abilities?

Obtained abilities will be capacities you acquire through training and experience. Frequently, gained abilities can incorporate both hard and delicate abilities, and these capacities might assist you with working on your presentation at work. Delicate abilities are not effectively quantifiable, yet they normally connect with how you deal with your work and team up and speak with others. Hard abilities frequently show that you have a specific specialised capacity, like programming or examining information.

Chapter 2

Finding a Profitable skills

The For sure Publication Group contains a different and gifted group of essayists, specialists and educated authorities outfitted with For sure's information and experiences to convey valuable tips to assist with directing your professional process.

To propel your profession, acquiring beneficial abilities can assist with separating you from different applicants. Having a created range of abilities draws in open positions and shows that you're able to do something beyond fundamental work obligations. Knowing which abilities are beneficial can assist you with figuring out which ones to create. In this article, we investigate what productive abilities are, instances of some, how to further develop them and beneficial abilities in the work environment.

Perceive how your compensation analyzes

Get customised compensation bits of knowledge with the To be sure Compensation Adding machine

What are beneficial abilities?

Productive abilities are those that range across different enterprises, positions and vocations, which assist experts with bringing in more cash inside their work area. They range from computerised advertising to relational abilities, and people can become familiar with these abilities through different assets, including formal schooling and online courses. A considerable lot of these abilities can assist with supporting the general pay an individual makes in a position and assist with separating them from the opposition. Assuming you're searching for abilities to propel your insight and increment your pay, mastering productive abilities is one method for doing as such.

10 instances of beneficial abilities

Coming up next are 10 instances of significant beneficial abilities you can use in the work environment:

1. Correspondence

Practically all positions require some type of correspondence. Having solid verbal and composed relational abilities can assist with separating you from different candidates and guarantee you're imparting really in the work environment. You might foster this expertise by taking a talking or composing course, or perusing a book with undivided attention.

2. Composing

In many positions, you might talk with staff and others through email or other composed correspondence. It might likewise assist you with keeping records and all the more successfully impart areas of progress with colleagues and administration. You can acquire these abilities in different ways, including through web-based composing courses and joining a local area composing studio bunch.

3. Website streamlining (Search engine optimization)

Site improvement has turned into undeniably famous expertise that businesses search for in applicants. Many organisations find Search engine optimization abilities profoundly significant since it's normal for organisations to perform errands and gain openness by utilising innovation. A few web-based courses offer Search engine, and optimization-based classes, to assist with propelling your insight around here.

4. Computerised advertising

Computerised showcasing involves advancing administrations and products, frequently over the web utilising promoting strategies or through an organisation's site. Organisations could find this expertise profoundly significant, which can enormously expand the compensation you procure in your situation. Think about taking a class or online course to propel your insight and comprehension of computerised promoting.

5. Public talking

On the off chance that you work in a place that requires public talking, for example, in gatherings or classes, propelling your public talking abilities can make your introductions fascinating and more obvious. You may likewise utilise this expertise to start your own beneficial business. Methods for further developing public talking incorporate perceiving your crowd and editing your discourse or show.

6. Innovation

With an ever-increasing number of organisations depending on innovation to maintain their organisations, innovation abilities have turned into a profoundly sought-after range of abilities that businesses search for in candidates. Instances of innovation abilities incorporate distributed computing, IT computerization, proactive security and equal figuring. You can acquire the majority of these abilities through an internet-based course, preparing workshop or advanced education establishment.

7. Project the board

Regardless of whether you're not a venture chief, learning project executives can assist with propelling your profession and show you how to lead groups in accomplishing objectives effectively. Instances of task the board abilities incorporate checking, executing, arranging and commencement. There are a few undertaking the executives' courses accessible to assist you with acquiring this range of abilities.

8. Unknown dialects

With the ceaseless development of globalisation and worldwide business, realising an unknown dialect can assist you with progressing inside your situation and furnish you with valuable open doors in nations across the world. A well-known position that requires unknown dialect information is that of an interpreter, with famous dialects to pick up including Italian,

Spanish and French. On the off chance that you work in a lawful, science or training field, you should seriously mull over concentrating on an unknown dialect.

9. Information science and examination

Information science and examination have turned into famous expertise among organisations as they keep on progressing in their innovation utilises. Information is significant in different businesses, with normal positions utilising information science, including examiners and researchers. Instances of information required for this expertise incorporate coding dialects and the utilisation of well-known projects, for example, Succeed.

10. HR

If you're hoping to get into general business the board, and human asset abilities are significant. These abilities incorporate specific administration abilities that permit human asset experts to manage colleagues and, surprisingly, human asset offices. You can acquire certificates and information in this ability through different web-based courses.

Step-by-step instructions to work on productive abilities

There are different ways you can work on your productive abilities, including a portion of the accompanying:

Hands-on preparing: A few organisations permit staff individuals to fan out from their ongoing jobs to master new abilities in different regions. Think about asking your association for preparing specific expertise on top of your ongoing obligations.

Online courses: Numerous web-based courses and projects can teach you a wide assortment of well-known and beneficial abilities. Consider exploring particular web-based courses by involving your favoured web search tool or asking somebody in your expert organisation.

Training: One more method for propelling your insight into productive abilities is to think about additional schooling. A few degrees centre explicitly around regions that

incorporate these abilities and permit you to carry out them in common sense settings.
Mentoring: You can master numerous abilities, such as communicating in an unknown dialect, by working with a confidential coach. Check whether you can find a mentor in your space who is a specialist in the language or other expertise you need to master.

There are different ways you can show and acquire beneficial abilities in the working environment. A portion of these techniques include:
Requesting that another colleague show you specific expertise in their leisure time
Asking about working in one more situation for a brief time frame so you can become familiar with the abilities related to the job
Inquiring as to whether they will pay for a web-based course or program that progresses your abilities in a specific region
Top quests for new employment close to you
Seasonal positions

Everyday positions
Telecommute occupations
Recruiting promptly occupations
View more positions Very on
Step-by-step instructions to feature productive abilities
Here are far to feature your productive abilities on your resumes and introductory letters:

Beneficial abilities for continue
Most continues contain an "abilities" segment that permits you to list your ongoing abilities that connect with the gig. Assuming you have productive abilities, make certain to incorporate these in your rundown. You can likewise incorporate your abilities and instances of how you've involved them in past positions in the "work insight" segment of your resume.

Beneficial abilities for an introductory letter
Many recruiting supervisors read an introductory letter before they get to the

resume, so including your productive abilities can assist with grabbing the attention of bosses and urge them to pursue. Consider remembering a couple of productive abilities for the second passage of your introductory letter. Give instances of how you've involved them before and how they've upheld your past positions.

Productive abilities for a prospective employee meeting

Most recruiting directors frequently ask about your abilities in a prospective employee meeting. Consider making a rundown of these abilities before going to the meeting so you remember to bring them up. Make certain to give instances of how you've involved these abilities in the past effectively.

Chapter 3

Monetizing your skill

Finding means to monetize your skills is one of the best methodologies to build your revenue source.

Notwithstanding, the subject matter you are energetic about will remain as a side interest except if you know how to produce pay out of it. That is the reason it is truly vital to recognize your abilities and what you are great at.
your advertising genuinely must incorporate something that will ignite their advantage and as well as feature the arrangement you can propose to your expected client's concern/s.

1. Do instructional exercise recordings on youtube

YouTube, as an online course, has a business opportunity for such material. On YouTube, individuals might bring in cash by sharing talented instructional exercises/master tips like inside brightening, humour, journaling, planting, procuring recurring, automated revenue, and some more (and so on). There are two different ways you can acquire recurring, automated revenue through youtube. What's more, this is through the promotion of livelihoods (paid coordinated efforts) and subsidiary showcasing.

2. Counselling/Instructing

If you have an attractive capacity that individuals are anxious to learn, it is one amazing method for procuring through training and counselling. From birthing, nurturing, instructing to showcasing training, there are plenty of different kinds of specialists. You'll presumably need to search for a client to work with from the beginning. Be that as it may, as your business extends and through a successful promoting and organising system, you are bound to acquire long-haul clients over the long haul. One of the stages I love to use for booking my counselling/training work is Dayslice. They have an exceptionally tasteful and slick stage that you can simply coordinate with any of your current virtual entertainment and course creation stages. Besides, their after-deals support is simply astounding.

3. Publishing content to a blog

Publishing content to a blog these days has been more popular than at any other time. You might bring in cash by publishing content to a blog in various ways. This could incorporate paid associations, brand-centred web journals, or potentially even as a professional writer (on the off chance that you compose a blog for another person). Just consistently keep your material zeroed in on a solitary subject. This will make it simple for individuals to grasp what's going on with your blog and for you to construct a readership. A portion of the devices I truly love concerning creating content for my web journals are Jasper.ai, copy.ai, and genei.io

4. Outsourcing

One of the clearest approaches to adapting your expertise is outsourcing. Numerous people are anxious to simply pay for your skill and administration. Pursue an outsourcing site, for example, Fiverr, Upwork or Freelancer Vets (on the off chance that you are a veteran or a tactical mate) to get everything rolling. These locales let you promote your administrations and simplify it for likely clients to find you.

5. Begin a Digital recording

If you are somebody who simply leaves talking and making advantageous discussions, facilitating your web recording is for you. For you to begin, ensure that you have plainly distinguished your specialisation and make an outwardly engaging site to act as your headquarters. You may likewise utilise virtual entertainment to promote your digital broadcast normally or through supported search systems, like Facebook, Instagram, Twitter, and different locales.

From the get-go, it tends to be hard to consider ways of adapting your abilities, however, it's worth the effort eventually. By carving out an opportunity to investigate various choices, you might observe that there are different ways for you to begin producing a pay from what you love. We trust this blog post has helped flash a few thoughts and given you a couple of beginning stages for making your maintainable second job.

Think adaptability!

Do you have at least some idea of what "think versatility" means?

It implies pondering approaches to selling your insight (which is likewise your item) to whatever number of individuals as could be allowed.

You might be an incredible educator and have a full timetable of classes, consistently. In any case, we possibly have 24 hours in a day and on the off chance that you show private English classes, you may have the option to show 24 illustrations per day - not thinking about, obviously, that you need to rest and eat. Furthermore, you will perhaps need to go in and out of town a ton if the classes are not all educated in a similar area. In this way, it would be humanly unimaginable for you to show every individual who needed to have classes with you, which thus would keep you from bringing in all the cash you could.
That is the reason the most straightforward approach to contacting many individuals and having the option to spread your insight

to the entire world is to exploit the potential outcomes the web gives.
With it, comes the market of computerised business ventures, answerable for making numerous business undertakings take off. What's more, the same thing can likewise happen to you.
Rather than offering homeroom illustrations, why not record video examples and make them accessible in a web-based course?
This sort of system isn't just accessible to instructors. A design specialist, for instance, can compose a total digital book on matching varieties and various outfits, very much like a painter can make a seminar on the best methods to paint walls without help from anyone else.

The web is hanging around for every individual who needs to instruct something. You simply have to sort out what the best organisation to circulate your insight is.
Benefits of computerised organisations

At the point when you deal with your computerised item, you can work from any place you need, and you'll just need a PC with web access. This is a significant benefit, particularly on the off chance that you wish to have additional opportunities to travel and accompany your loved ones.

Working for yourself will request more work, particularly proportional to your business quickly. Notwithstanding, the web is here to help us, and this incorporates computerised organisations.

You will want to computerise your business so it works for you, 24 hours every day, 7 days per week. Furthermore, you likewise have the chance of extending your business universally.

How to advance your work?

No matter how you decide to bring in cash from your gifts and abilities, you ought to continuously zero in on the most proficient method to draw in clients/understudies. All things considered, there's no utilisation in having an extraordinary item on the off chance that individuals don't arrive at your Business Page, or, in any event, when they do, they don't make the purchase.

There are numerous approaches to advancing your work and we have chosen the fundamental ones which assurance improved results:

Virtual Entertainment:
Facebook, Instagram, Twitter and other long-range informal communication locales are superb means to advance your work, particularly on the off chance that you have a dependable fan base and supporters. Pick the ones that best accommodate your speciality and crowd, and keep a consistent number of everyday posts. You really must keep up with consistency and consistently feed your online entertainment with content that can draw in your devotees.

Blog:

You can discuss nearly anything in web journals and this is a magnificent approach to showing the world what your identity is and what you do.

The thought, as we referenced prior, is to compose intriguing substance, which draws in the crowd with the profile you are focusing on, without referencing your organisation constantly.

For instance:

If you offer a seminar on getting thinner, expound on smart dieting, manners by which individuals can expand their satisfaction, and different subjects which will lead the crowd to your item normally.

Paid advertisements:
Google, Facebook, Twitter and different channels give space to individuals to publicise their items and administrations, paying an expense for it. These

advertisements are otherwise called supported joins.

The promotions are sectioned by your optimal crowd and with the highest-level watchwords that have a connection to your item or administration.

Email Showcasing:
Email promoting is a useful asset for you to talk straightforwardly to your crowd.

On the off chance that you have a site, give structures to the guests to leave their email addresses and get data straightforwardly to their inboxes.

You can send explicit messages to your endorsers, like a bulletin.

www.ingramcontent.com/pod-product-compliance
Lightning Source LLC
LaVergne TN
LVHW020537160826
845677LV00015B/4102

* 9 7 9 8 3 5 3 4 8 6 4 1 1 *